I0843296

ANIMAL COLORING BOOK FOR TODDLERS

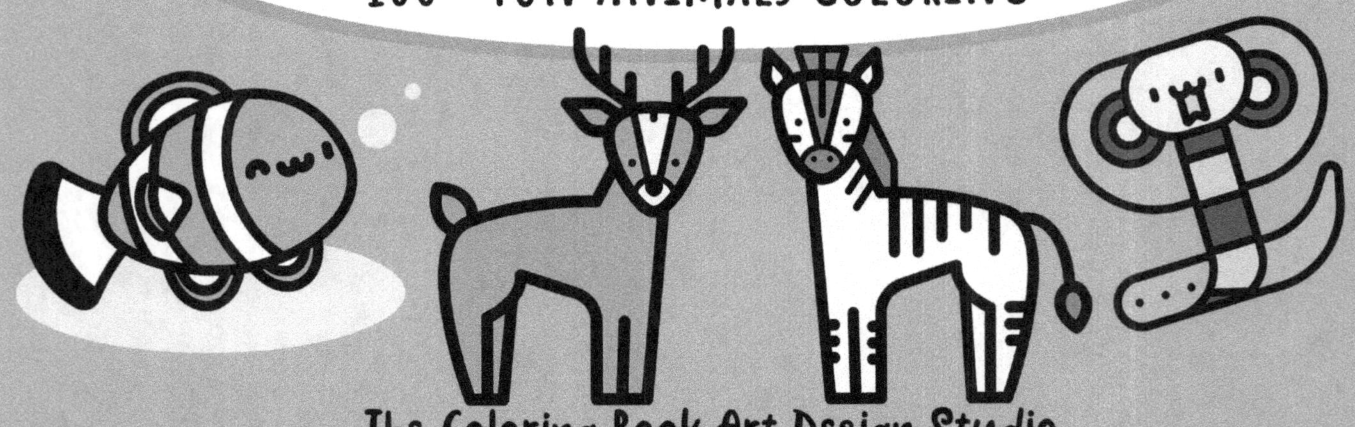

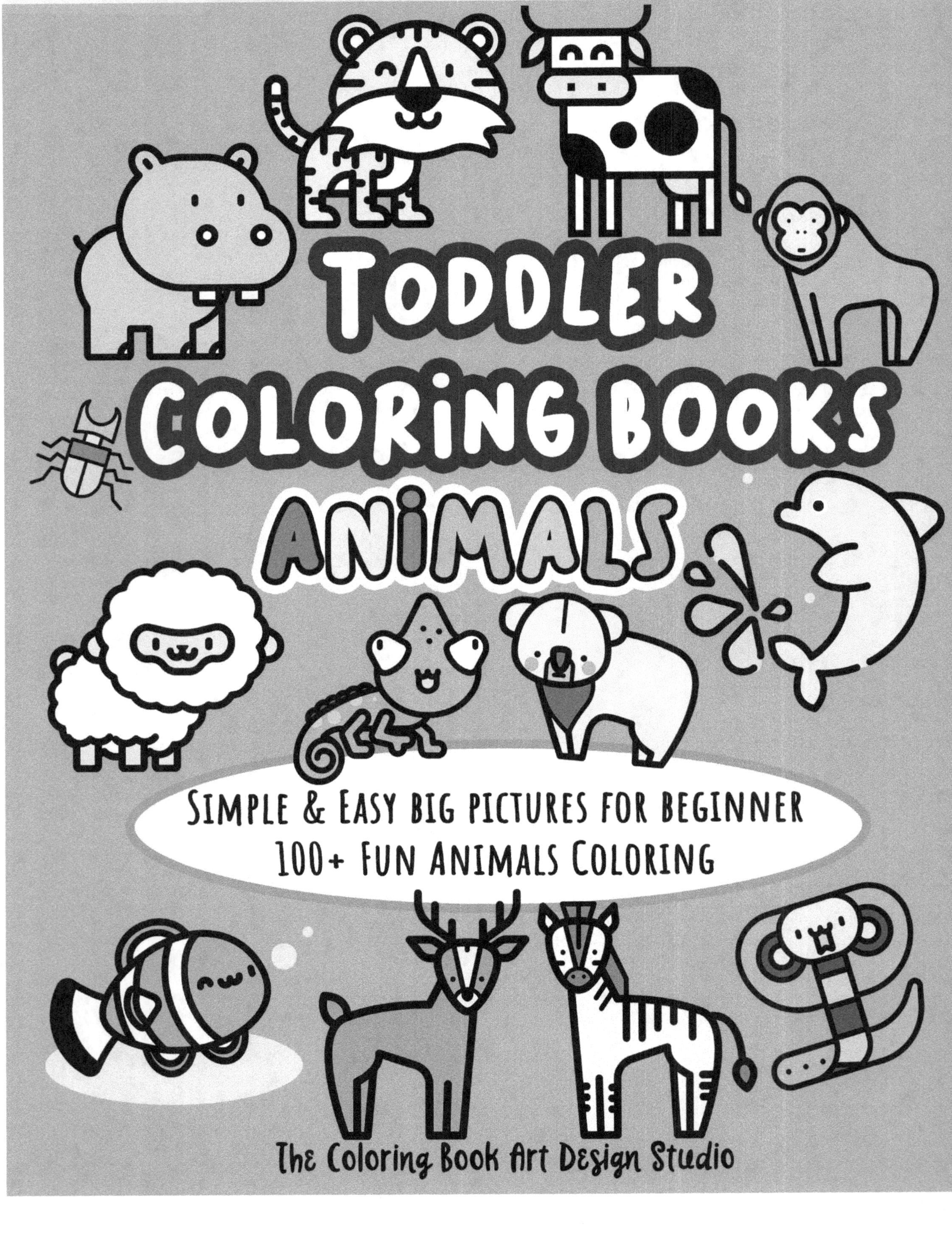
TODDLER
COLORING BOOKS
ANIMALS
SIMPLE & EASY BIG PICTURES FOR BEGINNER
100+ FUN ANIMALS COLORING
The Coloring Book Art Design Studio

Tiger

TODDLER
COLORING BOOKS ANIMALS

by The Coloring Book Art Design Studio

TODDLER
COLORING BOOKS ANIMALS

Zebra

THIS BOOK

BELONG TO

____

____

LET'S TEST YOUR COLOR

Aligator

Alpaca

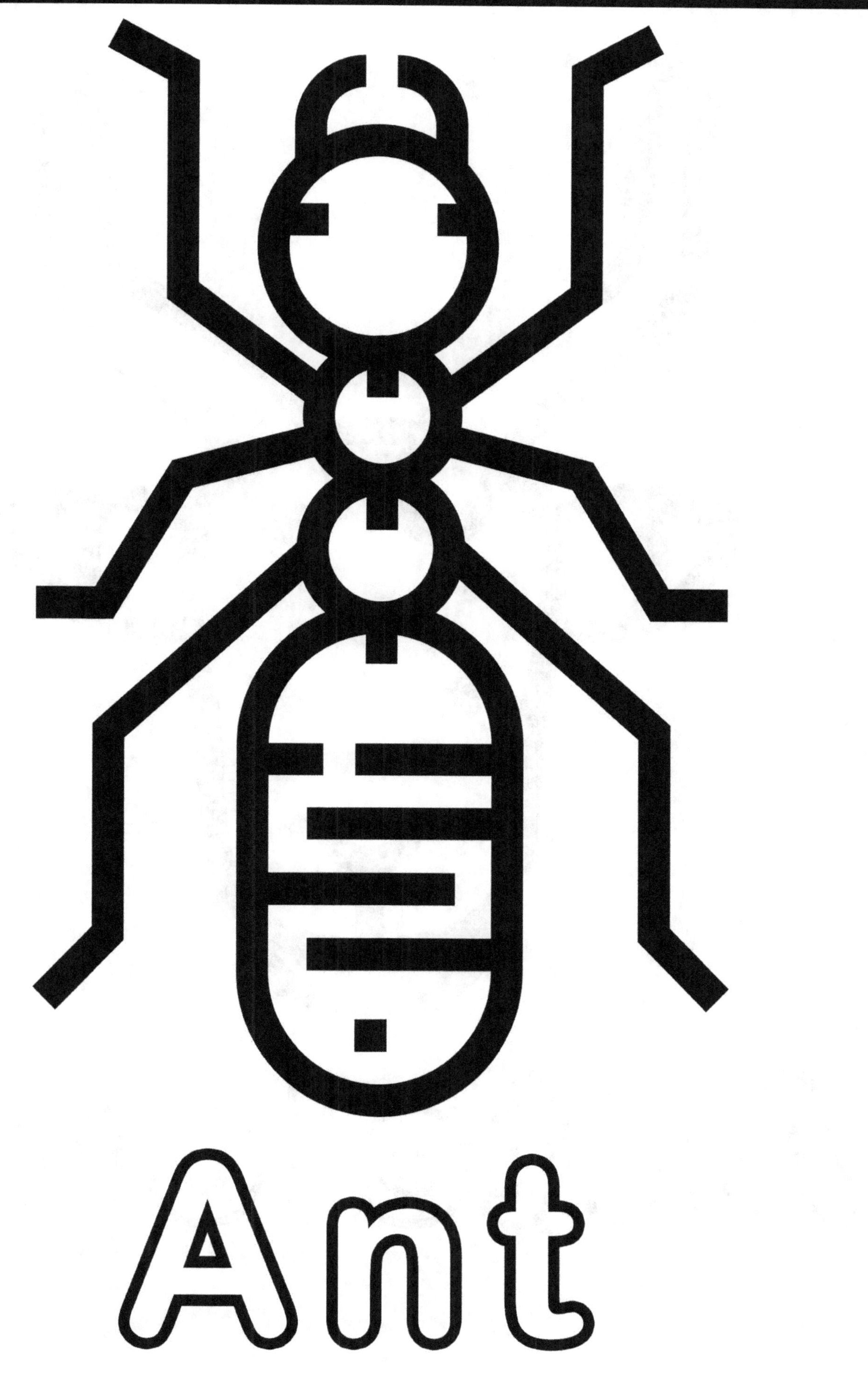

Ant

Antelope

Armadillo

Bat

Bear

Beaver

Bee

Beetle

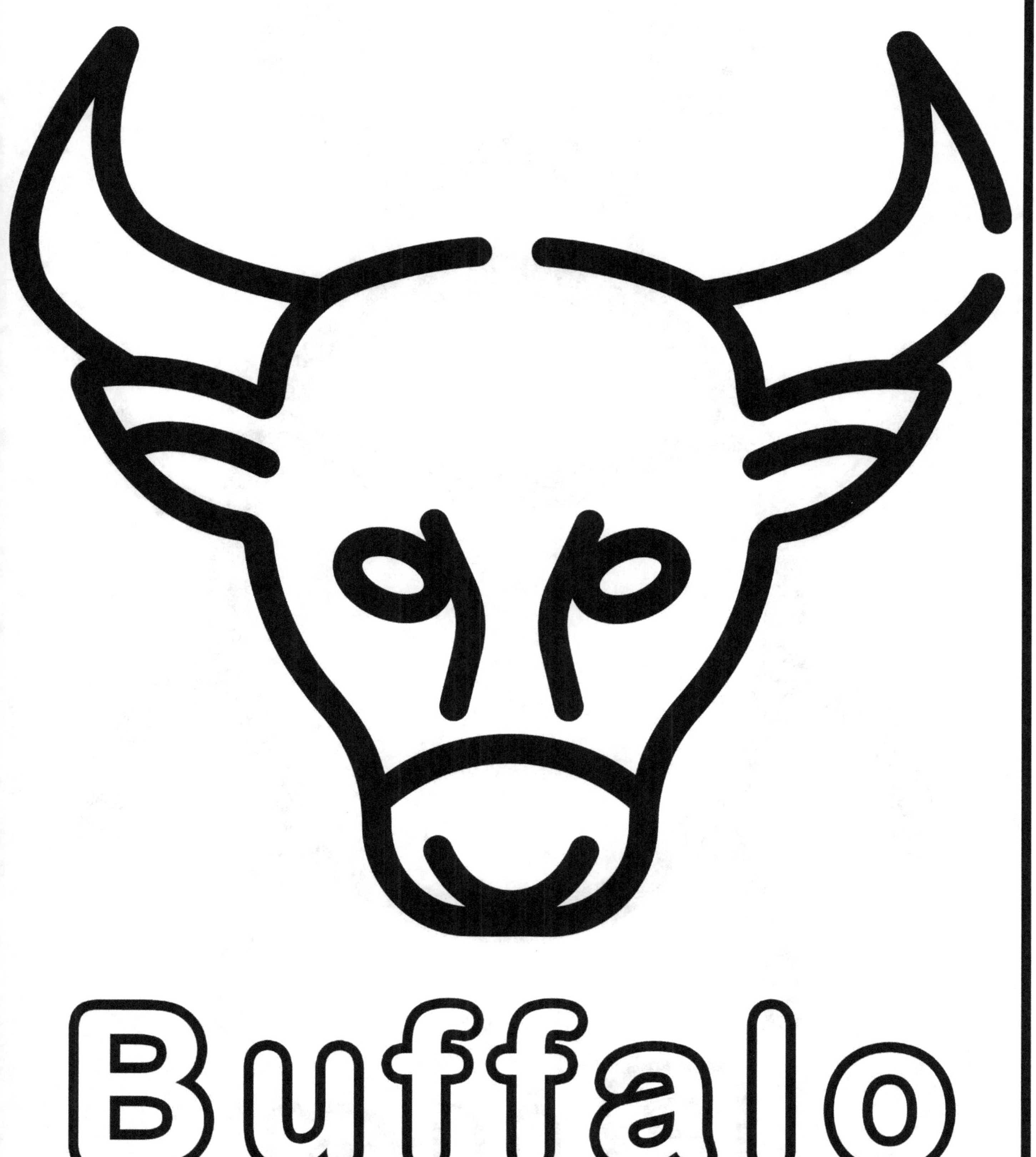

Buffalo

Bug

Butterfly

Camel

Cat

Chameleon

Cheetah

Chicken

Clam

Clownfish

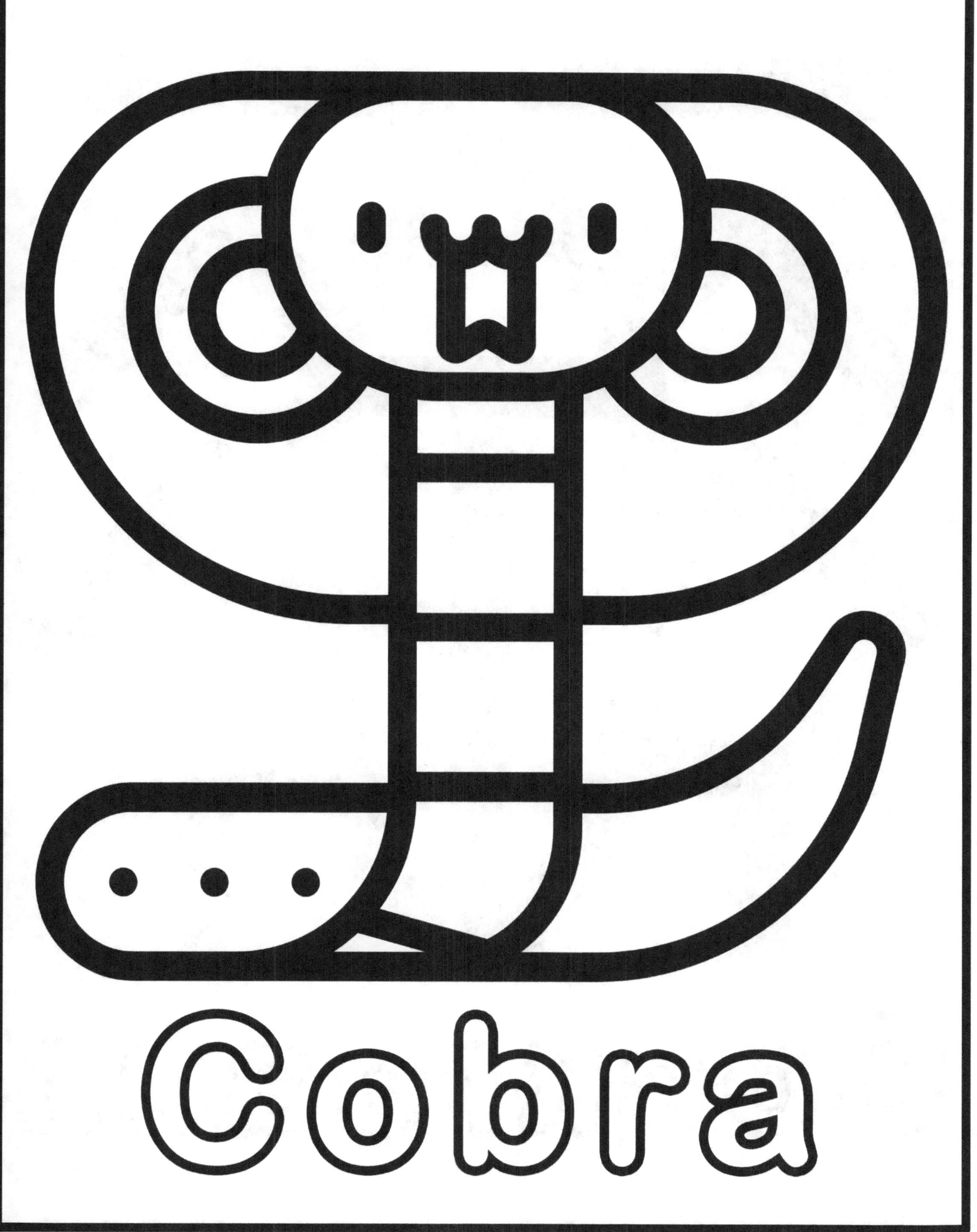
Cobra

Cockroach

Cow

Crab

Crow

Deer

Dinosaur

Dog

Dolphin

Dove

Dragon

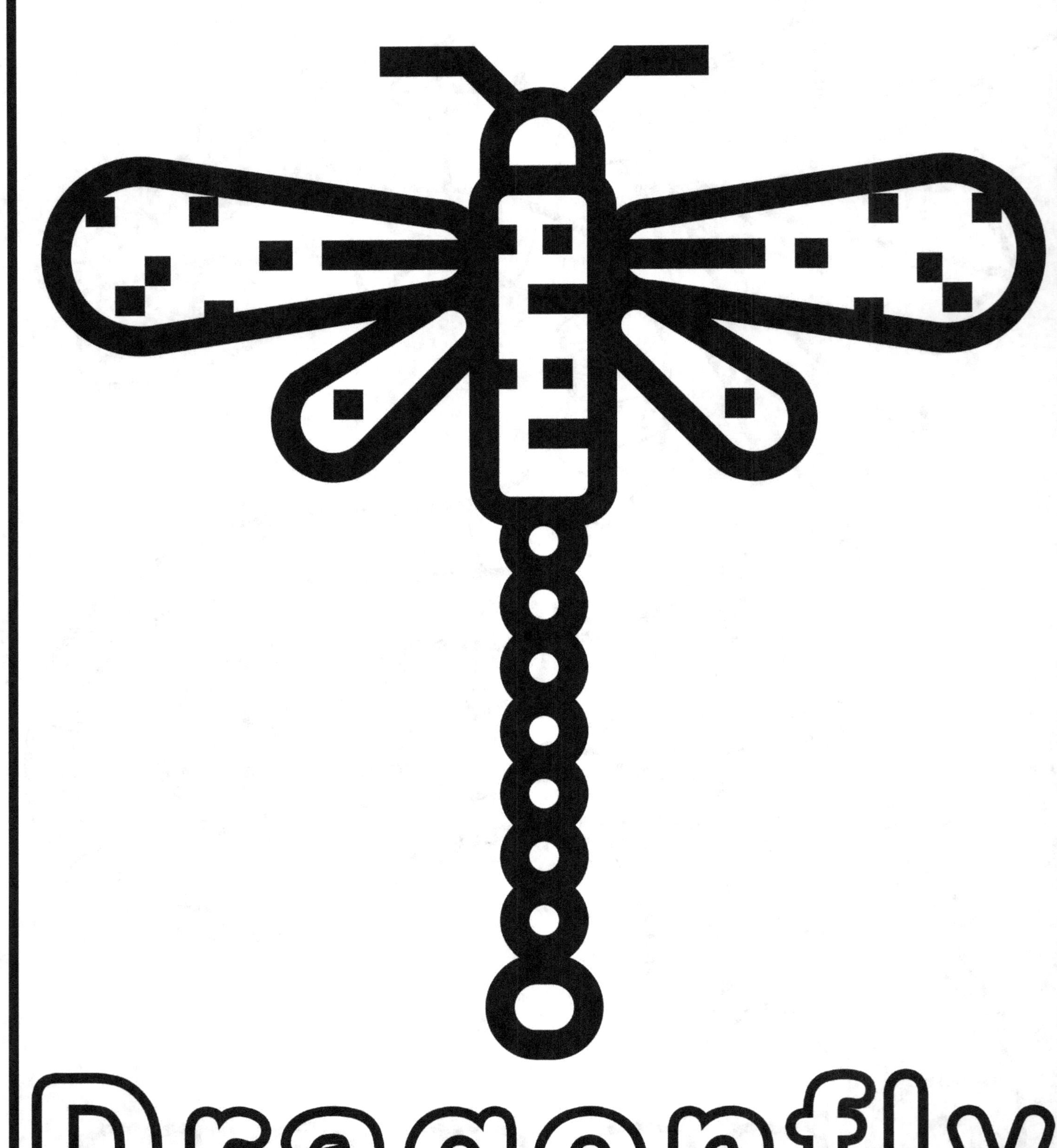

Dragonfly

Duck

Eagle

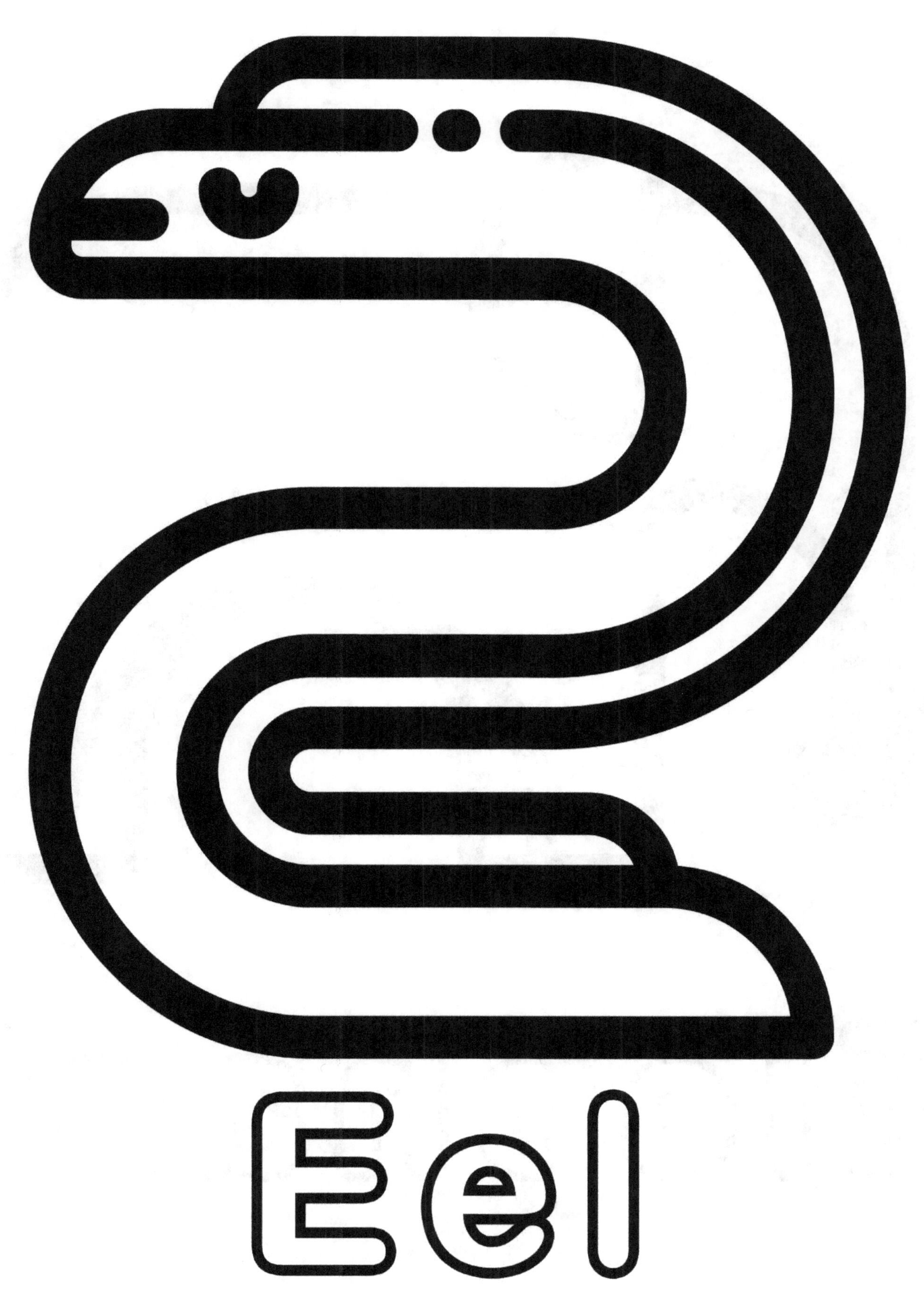

Eel

Elephant

Fish

Flamingo

Fox

Frog

Giraffe

Goat

Gorilla

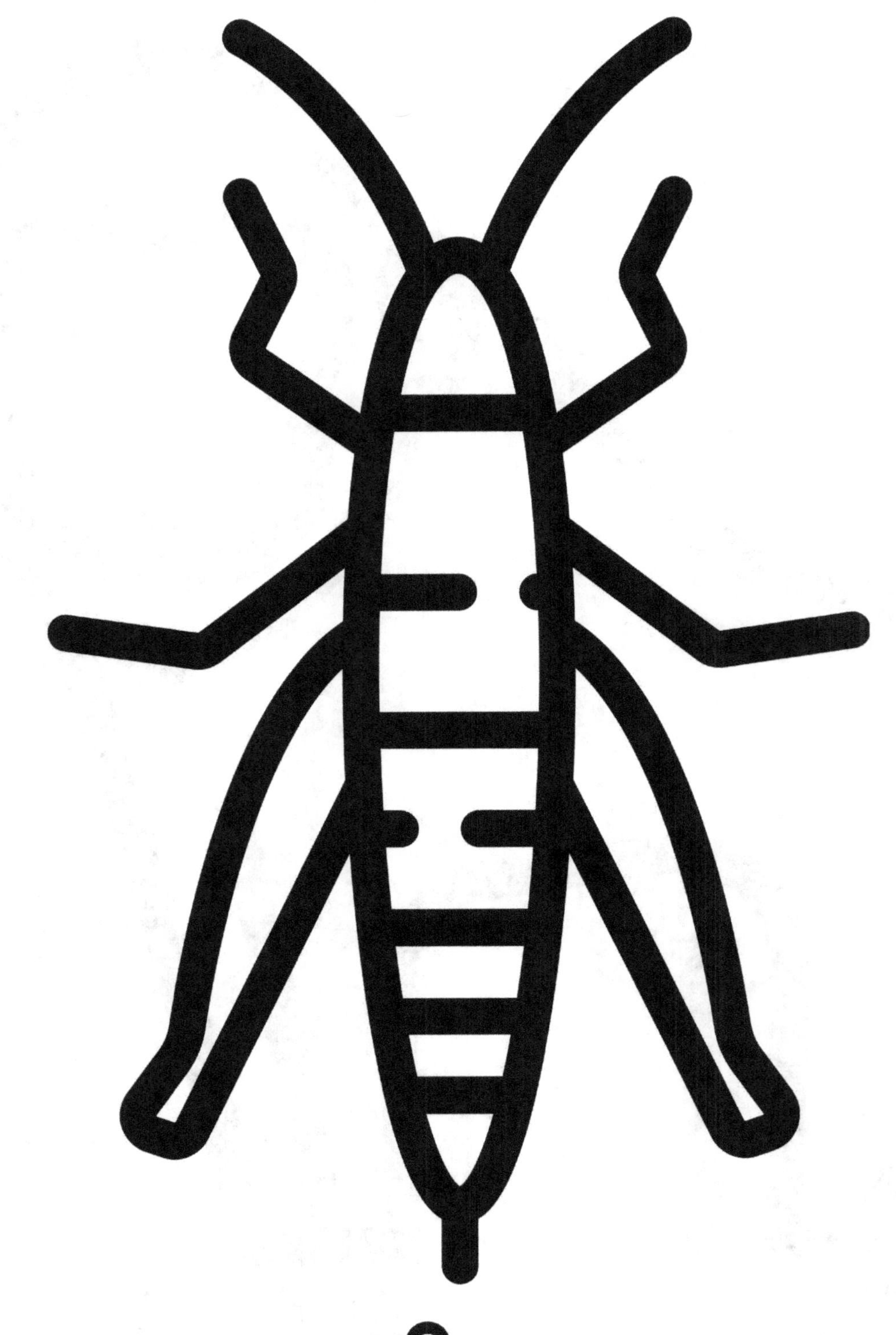

Grasshopper

Hamster

Hedgehog

Hippopotamus

Horse

Jelllyfish

Kangaroo

Koala

Ladybug

Leopard

Lion

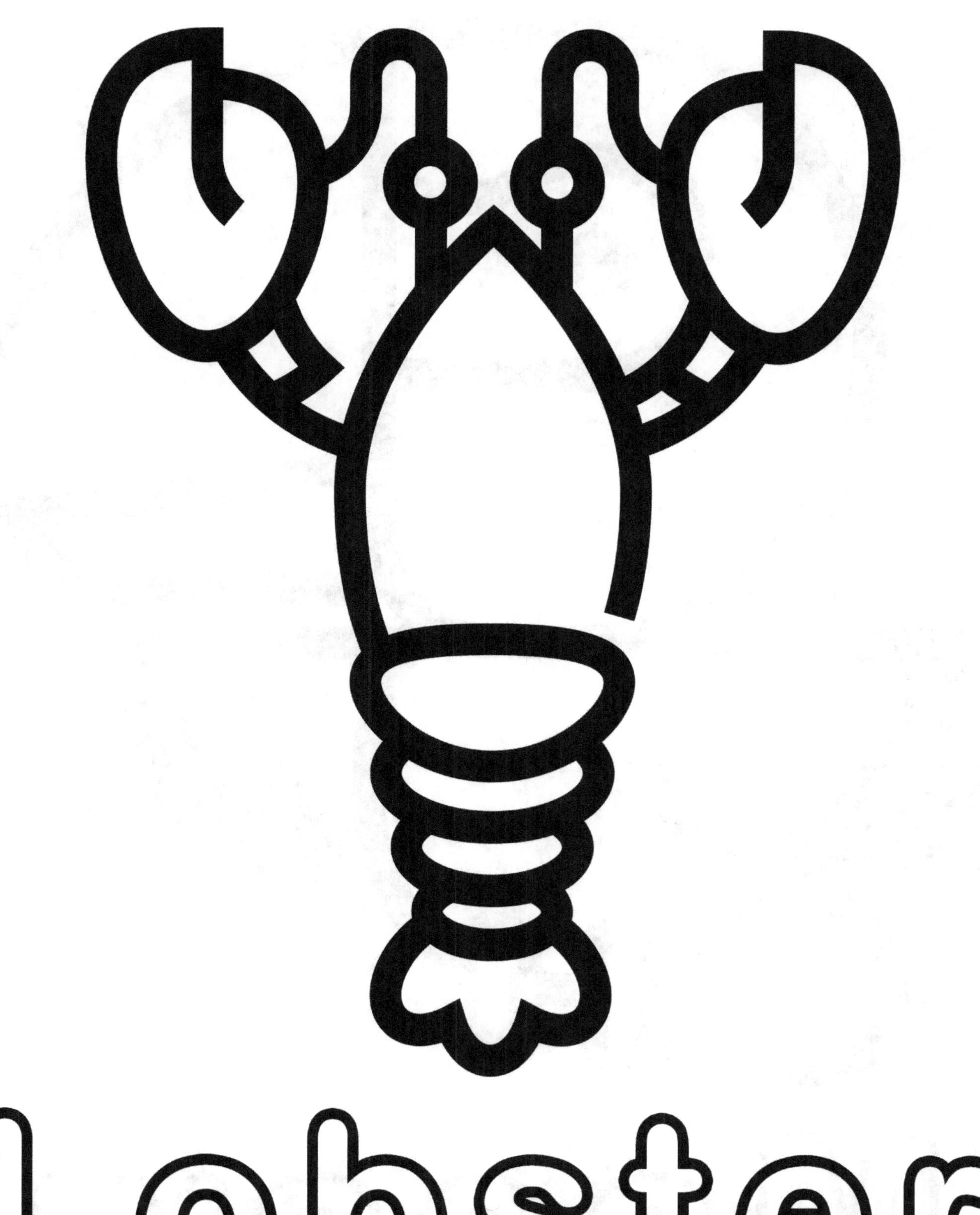

Lobster

Macaw

Mite

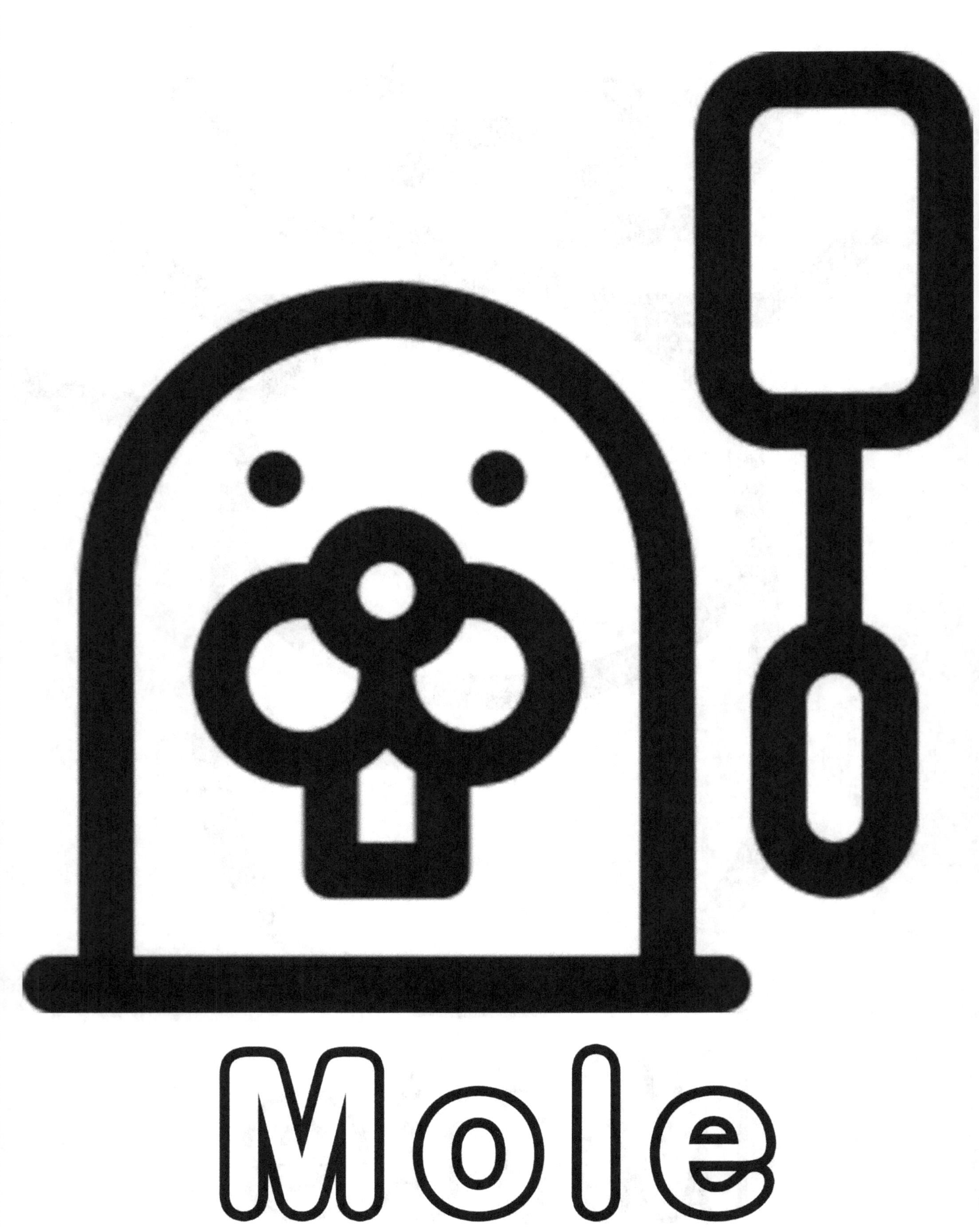

Mole

Monkey

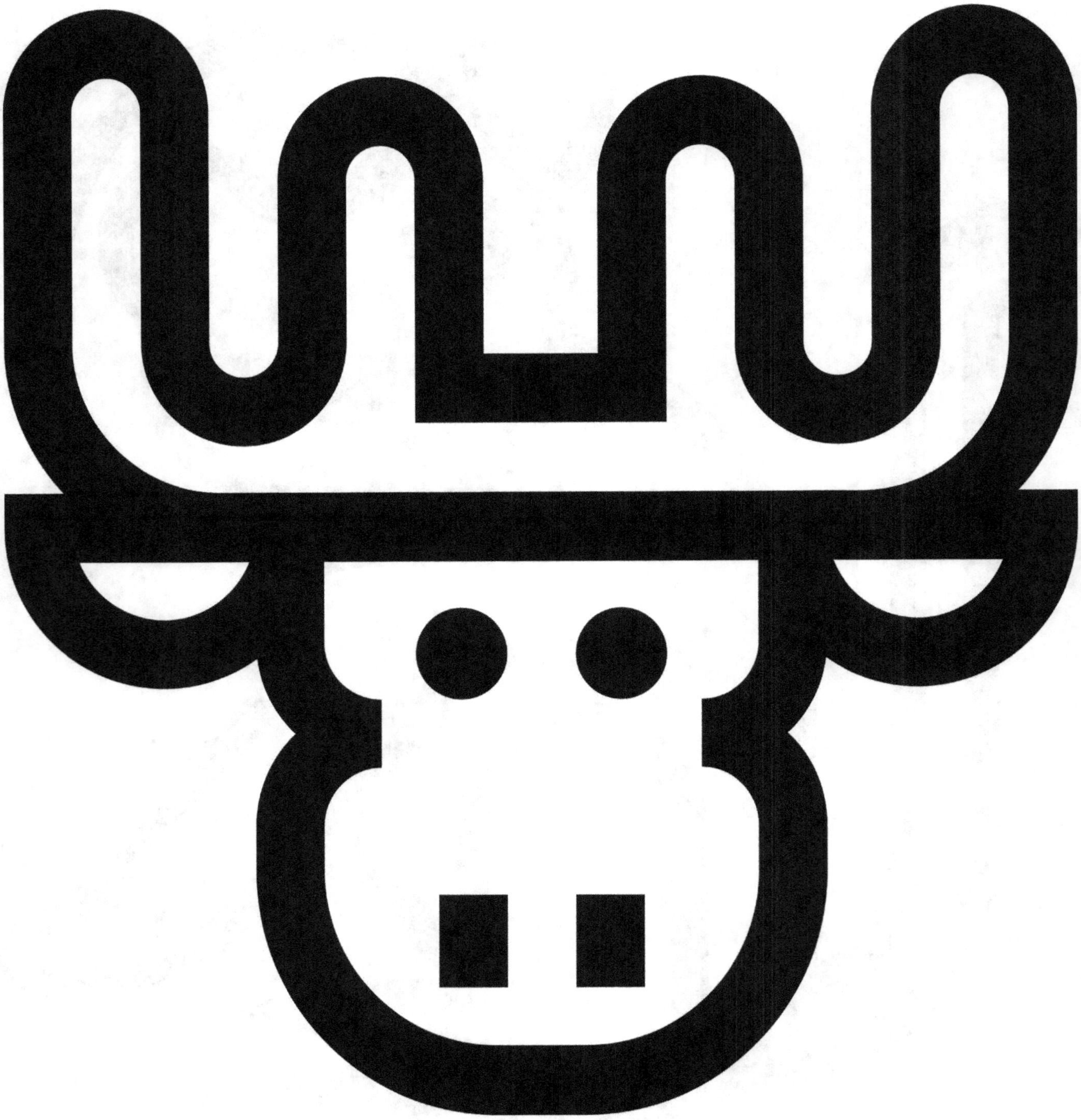

Moose

Mosquito

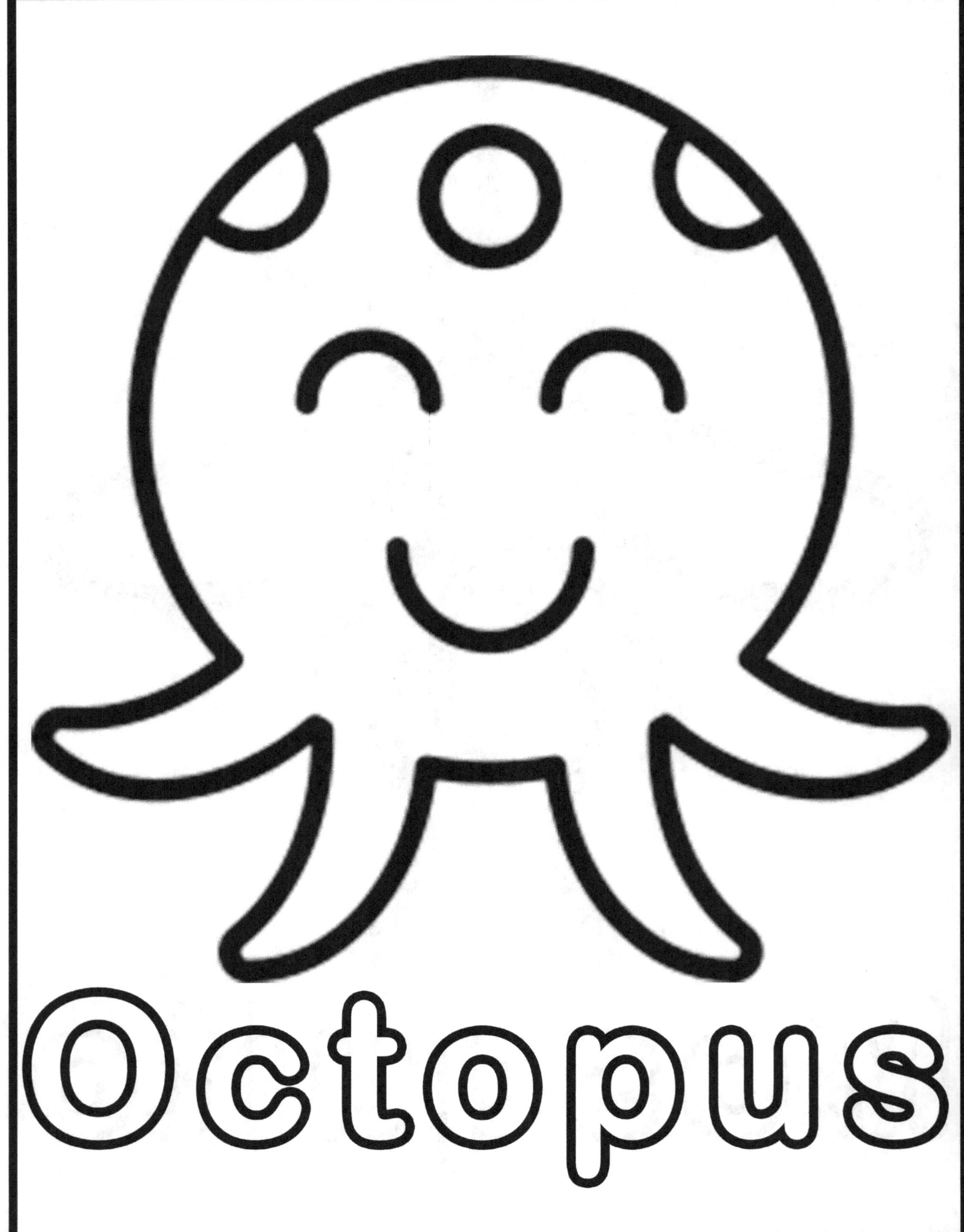

Octopus

Ostrich

Otter

Owl

Oyster

Panda

Parrot

Peacock

Penguin

Pig

Platypus

Pufferfish

Rabbit

Raccoon

Rat

Rhino

Rooster

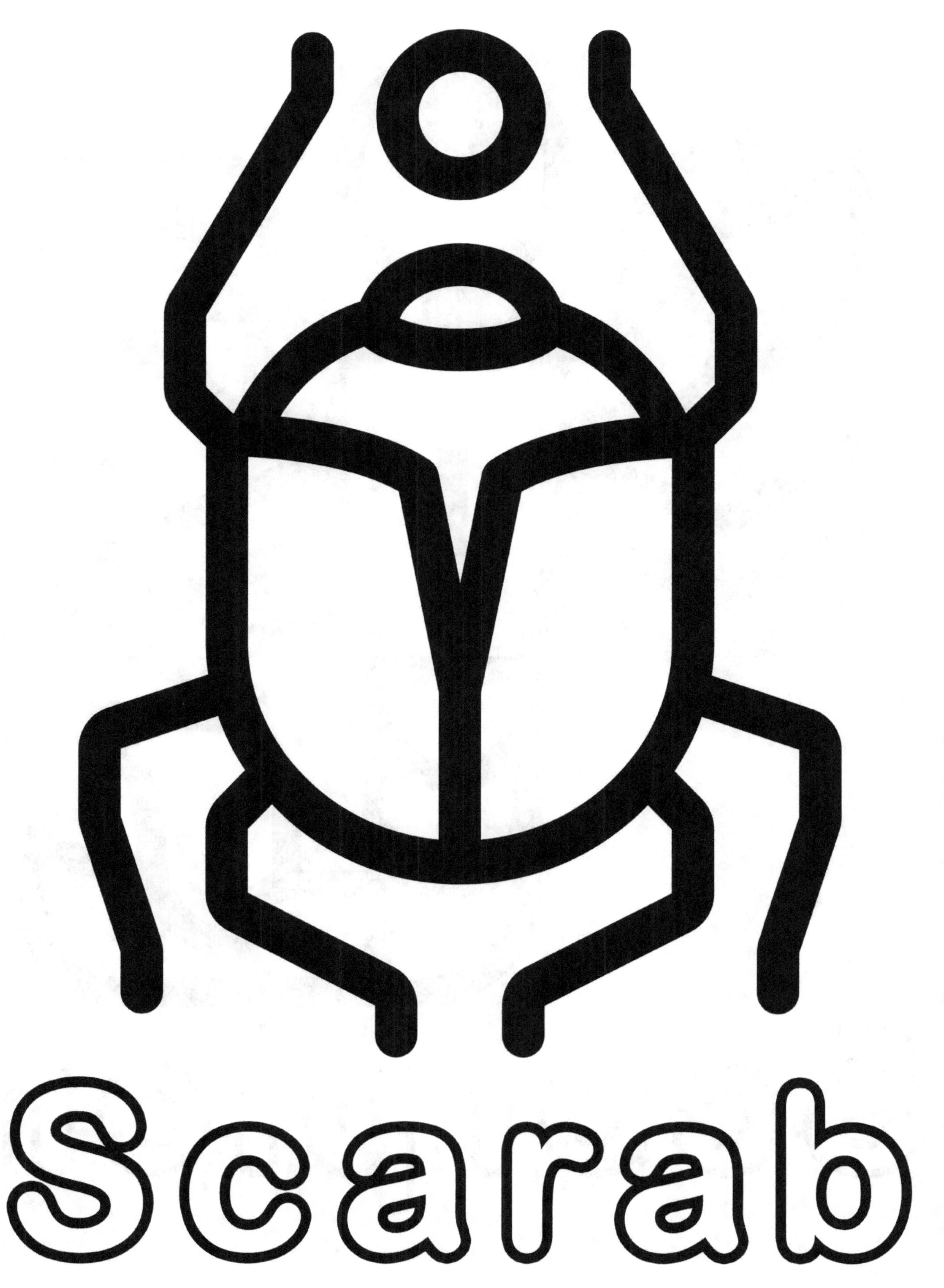

Scarab

Scorpion

Sea Lion

Seahorse

Shark

Sheep

Shrimp

Skunk

Sloth

Snail

Snake

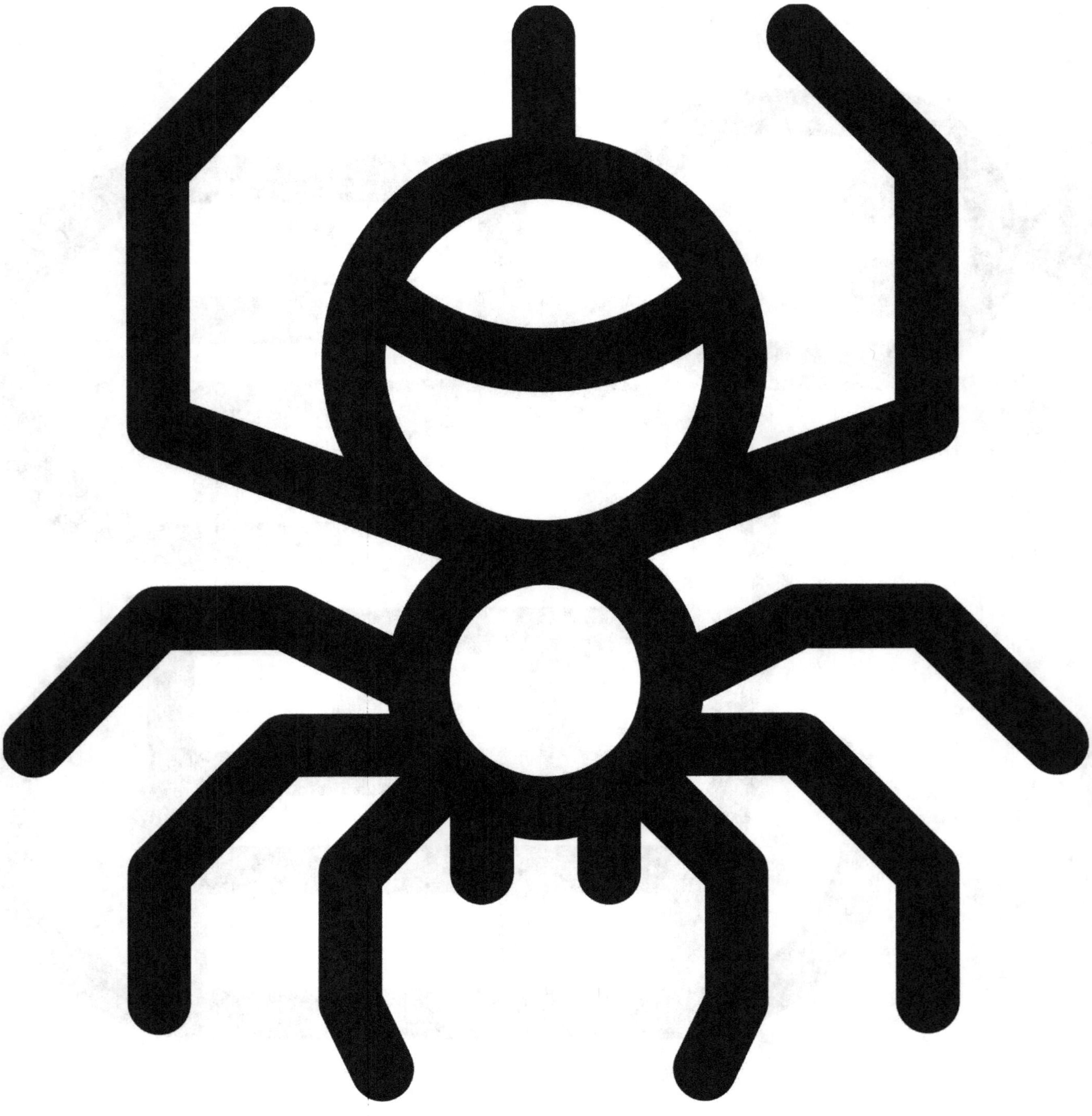

Spider

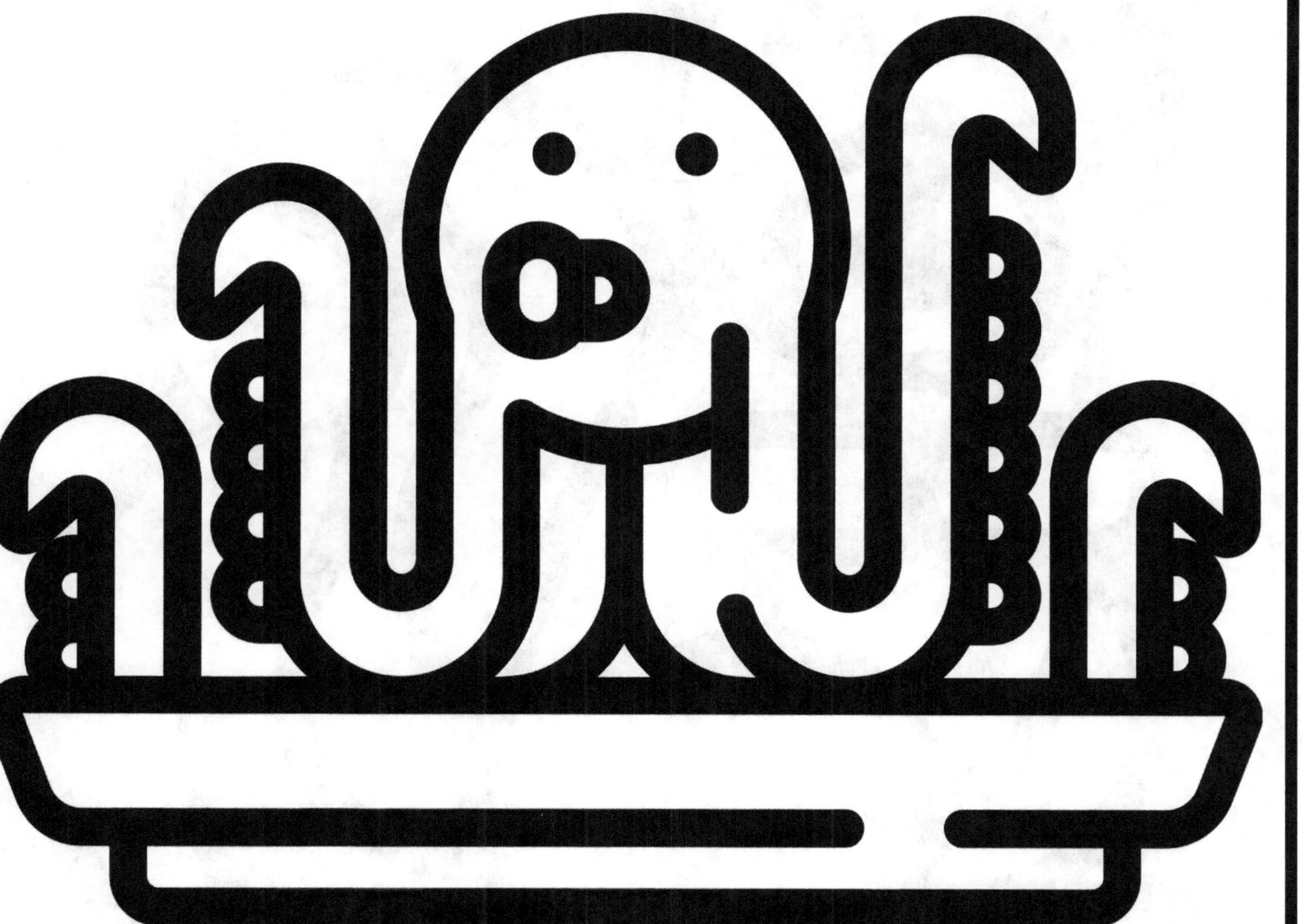

Squid

Squirrel

Swan

Swordfish

Tiger

Toucan

Turkey

Turtle

Unicorn

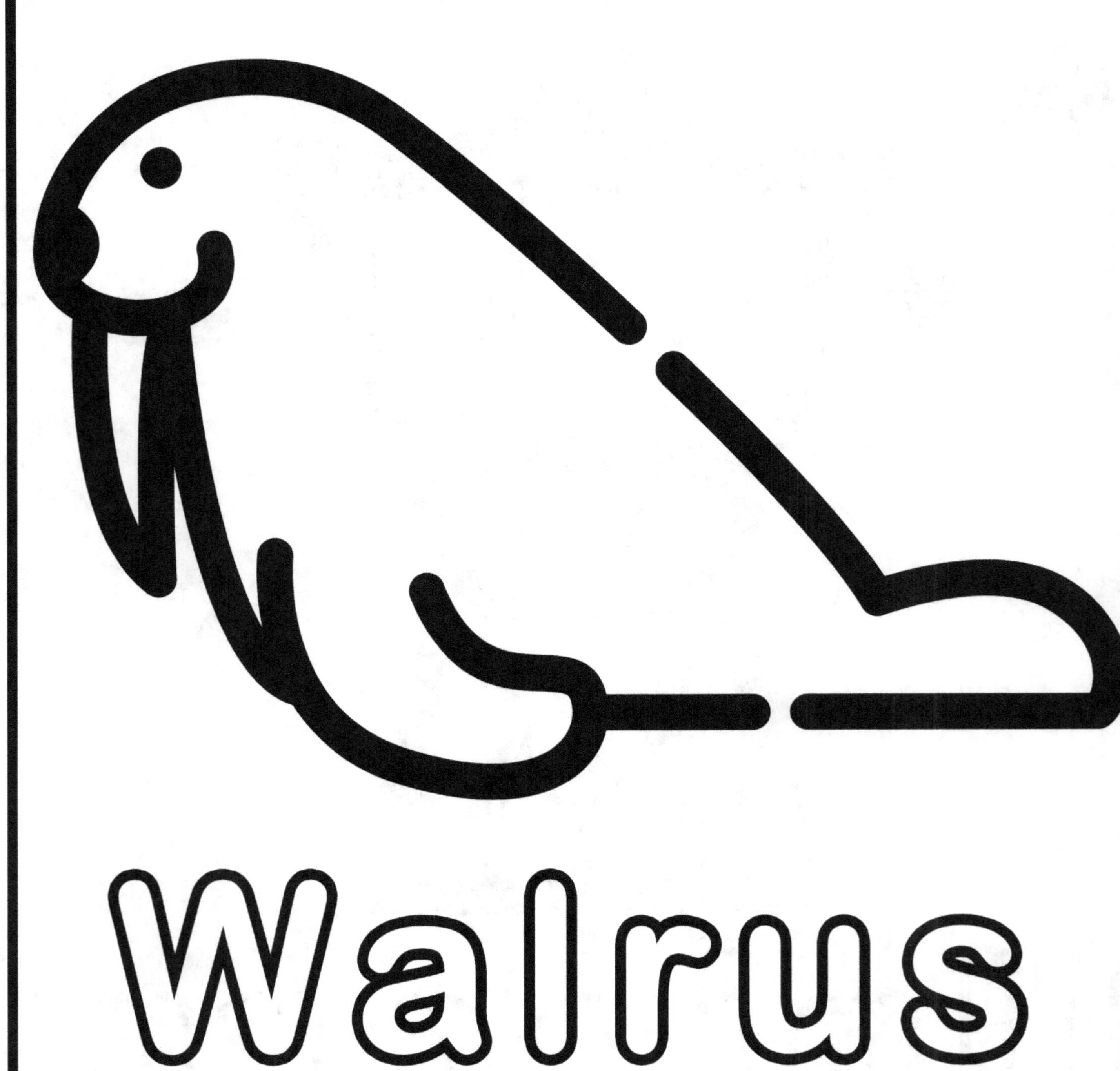

Walrus

Wasp

Whale

Wolf

Worm

Zebra